Hot Cocoa Comfort

Hot Cocoa Comfort

50 Recipes for Comforting Cups of Chocolate

Michael Turback

Skyhorse Publishing

Skyhorse Publishing books may be purchased in bulk at special discounts for sales promotion, corporate gifts, fund-raising, or educational purposes. Special editions can also be created to specifications. For details, contact the Special Sales Department, Skyhorse Publishing, 307 West 36th Street, 11th Floor, New York, NY 10018 or info@skyhorsepublishing.com.

Skyhorse® and Skyhorse Publishing® are registered trademarks of Skyhorse Publishing, Inc.®, a Delaware corporation.

Visit our website at www.skyhorsepublishing.com.

10 9 8 7 6 5 4 3

Library of Congress Cataloging-in-Publication Data is available on file.

Cover design by Mona Lin
Cover photo courtesy of iStock
Interior design by Chris Schultz

Print ISBN: 978-1-5107-3996-3
Ebook ISBN: 978-1-5107-3997-0

Printed in China

Contents

·······················

Introduction: Life in a Cup

Animal crackers, and cocoa to drink, That is the finest of suppers, I think. When I'm grown up and can have what I please, I think I shall always insist upon these.

—Christopher Morley

Oh, comfortable cocoa! There are few indulgences in life more easily obtained. Cocoa is a simple pleasure during any season of life, at any moment in daily life, and for life's special occasions.

The story begins with ancient Mayans, rulers of what is now the Mexican Yucatan and Guatemala, who domesticated the cocoa tree, roasted and pounded its beans into a grainy liquid, added seasonings, and placed the nourishing beverage at the center of their fantastic civilization. When Spanish conquistadors arrived to plunder riches of the New World early in the 16th century, they discovered treasuries stockpiled, not with silver or gold, but with cocoa beans.

Tempered with sugar and spices to suit European tastes, what became known as "chocolate" emerged as the fashionable libation of lords and ladies. They sipped the drink from deep, straight-sided cups, while members of royalty flaunted their wealth by drinking from golden chalices. By the time drinking chocolate made its way to the British Isles, milk had been added to the mixture, and, although chocolate houses flourished in major cities, the steaming cup was still very much a privilege of society's upper crust.

Hot chocolate was most closely associated with the aristocratic bedroom, as it was popular to drink first thing in the morning as well as in the evening before going to sleep. A painting by French artist Jean-Baptiste Le Prince from 1769 depicts a woman lying in bed, reaching out for her departed lover, the morning light illuminating her figure. A chocolate pot and cups sit by her bedside.

In 1828, everything changed. Casparus van Houten, proprietor of a chocolate factory in Amsterdam, invented and patented a hydraulic press that extracted the "butter" from roasted cocoa beans to create a "cake." It was then pulverized and sieved through mesh silk to produce a smooth, soft, uniform powder. The van Houten method led to the mass production and consumption of cocoa, or, as some have pronounced, the "democratization" of chocolate.

After visiting an exhibition of innovative German-made chocolate-producing machines at the Chicago World's Fair in 1893, a young American confectioner by the name of Milton Snavely Hershey purchased every single piece of equipment on display. Within a few months, his plant in Lancaster, Pennsylvania, was grinding cocoa powder for drinking and baking, and Hershey's Cocoa quickly became the first nationally marketed product of its kind. Thanks to Mr. Hershey, the warm, filling, comforting qualities of cocoa became an essential staple in American life.

Yet as time moved toward the present, paled by comparison to the beverages consumed in an ever more caffeinated culture, cocoa lost some of its appeal, considered the mundane alternative to *lattes*, cappuccinos, macchiatos, and other such things. To make matters more confusing, Americans have come to use the terms "hot chocolate" and "hot cocoa" interchangeably, obscuring the considerable difference between the two. European-style hot chocolate or drinking chocolate tends to be richer and more intense than its gentle, powdery relative, hot cocoa.

Everyday comfort is grounded in memories of that tin of cocoa in grandma's kitchen, where life was better inside a warm sweater and slow food was a practice, not a movement. Best of all, rediscovery is in the air—what once was old is new again.

This book invites the reader to reconsider the gentle but deep, complex flavor and amazing versatility of pure, natural cocoa as a return to our culinary roots and reconnection with one of the good things in life.

Finding comfort has been a human pursuit since the beginning of time. A warm cup of stovetop hot cocoa practically requires an unhurried moment; it begs to be sipped quietly, savored as a treat that kindles feelings of safety and innocence while it gently warms the heart and lifts the spirits. The humble cup, taken in leisure, offers a change of pace from the fast lane. Life can never feel rushed while sipping cocoa, either alone or with friends. The slowness of the ritual makes it more profound and more valuable. According to Gandhi, "There is more to life than increasing its speed."

The time may come when you make the simple pleasure of hot cocoa part of your daily life. When that moment graces you, and it will, it's a wondrous thing.

The Cocoa Kitchen

Cocoa Powder

Cocoa powder is made by extracting most of the cocoa butter richness from chocolate liquor (ground roasted cocoa beans) and pulverizing the dry residue.

There are two types of cocoa: natural (nonalkalinized) and Dutch process (alkalinized). Natural cocoa powder (also called unsweetened) is simply untreated cocoa powder. It's lighter and slightly more astringent, with almost citrusy notes. Dutch process cocoa has been treated with an alkali to make the powder more soluble. Along the way, "dutching" gives the cocoa a deep mahogany color and a smoother, earthier, "Oreo cookie" flavor. (If you're using soy or skim milk, Dutch process may minimize the chance of curdling.)

The most popular American brands of cocoa powder contain about 7% cocoa butter, while specialty and European cocoa powders contain 12 to 24% cocoa butter. Some products are cocoa powder alone, while some may include artificial flavors, nonfat dry milk, preservatives, soy lecithin, vanilla, and sugar.

Note: In English-speaking countries, the word "cacao" came to be pronounced "cocoa," and "cocoa powder" called simply "cocoa." As a result, many people assume that cocoa powder is just the ground beans themselves, and that chocolate is made from cocoa powder, instead of the other way around.

Mexican Chocolate

An authentic Mexican-style hot cocoa can be made from a hockey puck-shaped tablet of coarsely-ground chocolate, laced with cinnamon and sugar. Each tablet is divided into eight wedge-shaped segments that break off as needed for recipe portions. These rustic chocolates are available in Mexican markets, some supermarkets, or from online merchants. Abuelita, Ibarra, and Taza are common brands to look for.

Milks

Hot cocoa can be made with any milk-like beverage, dairy or nondairy. Deciding between whole, skim, or low-fat milk is a matter of personal choice in terms of diet, use, and preference. Skim or low-fat milk might be a better choice for people who are trying to hit specific daily caloric goals or those who already obtain a lot of fat from other foods in their diet. Vegans and others may prefer to drink plant- or nut-based milks over cow's milk. These milks have sweet, nutty flavors that blend beautifully with cocoa and produce wonderfully rich results.

Never let your milk actually come to a boil. This will preserve peak cocoa flavor and avoid scalding or curdling the milk. Soymilk and skim milk should be heated particularly gently; heat combined with the natural acidity in cocoa make them more susceptible to curdling.

Sweeteners

Homemade cocoa has all the delicious chocolate taste and none of the preservatives and additives that may be in a mix purchased in a grocery store. Prepared cocoa mixes often contain more sugar than cocoa, so always start with unsweetened cocoa powder and add a little sugar or other sweetener as desired.

Sugar adds sweetening, volume, and texture to hot cocoa. Although granulated white sugar is most commonly used, other sugars and sweeteners can add a new life to your drink.

Granulated white sugar or "table sugar" has medium-sized granules. When heated, granulated sugar takes on toffee-like color and flavor.

Confectioner's sugar, which has been crushed mechanically (and generally mixed with a little starch to keep it from clumping), is favored for its dissolving properties, especially in an iced cocoa drink.

Brown sugar is simply white sugar with a bit of molasses to give texture and color. Its color will depend on the amount of molasses added during processing. The darker the color the stronger the taste, so use one that suits your taste preference. Substituting brown sugar for white sugar in a hot cocoa recipe will add notes of butterscotch and molasses.

Sucanat is organically grown, freshly-squeezed sugar cane juice, clarified, filtered, and evaporated. The syrup is then crystallized and granulated into sugar. Sucanat flavor is quite extraordinary, and it adds a layer of caramel flavor to hot chocolate.

For even deeper flavor, use Muscovado sugar. Darkest of the raw dark brown sugars, muscovado has a fine-grained texture with natural molasses to provide a strong, lingering flavor that can't be matched by any regular brown sugar you would find in a grocery store.

Spices

They are the dried roots, barks, berries, and other fruits of tropical seeds. Spices are among the earliest commodities to have crossed the globe in trade networks. These powerful, lyrical, sensual aromatics have imparted their goodness to chocolates for thousands of years. Whether traditional or unfamiliar, thoughtful pairings seamlessly combine for a nurturing, soothing, and satisfying experience, and the aroma from the simmering mixture of milk, cocoa, and spices can be absolutely amazing.

For best results, buy small quantities of ground spices and store them in tightly-closed containers in a cool, dark, and dry place for no longer than a year. Before using, sniff. If the fragrance of a spice has dimmed, toss it out. Chances are the flavor has weakened as well and will do nothing to improve the drink.

Store vanilla beans completely submerged in granulated sugar. While that process preserves the moisture and freshness of the beans, it also creates an aromatic vanilla sugar that can be used for baking.

As a general rule, cocoa preparations should include a pinch of salt (approximately ⅟₁₆ teaspoon). Salt deepens the flavor and enhances the perceived sweetness of the cocoa. Kosher salt's slightly larger crystals have a more pinch-able, easy-to-control texture.

Tools/Accessories

Measuring cups and spoons, a pot or two, and a wooden spoon are the basic kitchen utensils you'll need to prepare hot cocoa. Set aside a few bowls and/or your set of cups for serving.

Cooking

The favored method for cooking hot cocoa is as simple as stirring cocoa powder with hot milk in a non-reactive pan. Heat the milk over medium-low heat, and be sure to remove the pan from the heat just before it reaches the boiling point. Overheating milk destroys the flavor and texture.

Always add wet to dry (instead of dry to wet) to prevent lumps. Place dry ingredients (cocoa, sugar, and salt) in the cup or pot, then add a very small amount of hot milk and stir until you have a paste—a wooden spoon will do the job. The heat will make it easier to dissolve the cocoa powder. Gradually stir in more and more milk to thoroughly blend, making sure to *scrape corners*. (If you missed any lumps, whisk to break them up.)

Always treat cocoa with respect in order to ensure the best result.

Mixing/Frothing

Some like it frothy. The more air you can get into hot cocoa, the more creamy smoothness and lighter consistency you'll impart to the drink. As soon as it comes off the stove, beat vigorously with a wire whisk, immersion blender, or old-fashioned egg beater until the surface of the drink is covered with foam.

Toppings

With a light, sweet fluffy cloud of whipped cream floating on top, hot cocoa is transported to higher ground. Do not settle for processed canned whipped topping. Take a few minutes and blend your own heavy cream. Real whipped cream is rich and decadent and its flavor is superior to that of its artificial counterparts. For a special treat, flavor the cream with your choice of delicious ingredients.

Marshmallows add a touch of whimsy to hot cocoa (see recipe on page 115).Use a kitchen torch to carefully toast marshmallows until they're evenly browned, with not much charring along the edges. If you don't have a kitchen torch, turn on your oven broiler and place the tray of marshmallows on a rack about six inches beneath the flame, watching them carefully as they toast.

Serving

A wide-mouth cup or mug will optimize the *aroma* and *flavor* experience of hot cocoa. Prewarming the cup or mug will slow the cooling of the drink. Fill with simmering water. Let stand for a few minutes, then empty, dry, and refill with hot cocoa.

The drink is best served hot off the stove, so the first sips should be taken from a spoon. Studies have concluded that 136°F. is the ideal temperature for drinking hot cocoa.

How to Make a Perfect Cup

Obligatory Hot Cocoa
Cinnamon-Infused Hot Cocoa
Chantilly Cream
Frozen Hot Cocoa
Melted Ice Cream Hot Cocoa
Hot Cocoa, Mexican Style

Obligatory Hot Cocoa

Regular consumption is the most typical characteristic of cocoa drinkers. A heart-warming cup has become an ordinary—in the best sense of the word—part of their daily lives. A few simple ingredients combine to create a rich and creamy hot cocoa that tastes better than anything sold in a package at the store. Always begin with unsweetened cocoa powder—that more than anything improves the hot cocoa experience. A little experimentation will establish how much sweetener you like best. Then decide on the milk of your choice. Before serving, use an immersion blender to create a luxurious froth in just a matter of seconds.

2 rounded teaspoons unsweetened cocoa
1 level teaspoon sugar, or to taste
1 pinch salt
1 cup milk

Combine cocoa powder, sugar, and salt in your favorite cup. Place milk in a small saucepan over medium heat until it becomes hot, not quite to a boil. Add just a few tablespoons of the hot milk into the cocoa mix, and stir into a smooth paste. Gradually add the remainder of the milk and continue stirring until fully incorporated. Froth with an immersion blender until creamy and foamy.

Makes 1 serving

Cinnamon-Infused Hot Cocoa

Its name is derived from the ancient Hebrew, meaning "sweet wood." Considered "the chief of all spices," aromatic cinnamon was pursued by ancient civilizations for perfumes, incense, and oils, referenced in the Bible as an "earthly treasure." Use true Ceylon cinnamon to add sweetness, complexity, and deep, enchanting fragrance—cocoa is pleasurable, and cinnamon enhances that pleasure. It also adds a dash of good health; cinnamon has been shown to lower bad cholesterol and boost cognitive function and memory.

½ cup unsweetened cocoa
2 tablespoons sugar, or to taste
½ teaspoon ground cinnamon + extra for dusting
1 pinch salt
4 cups milk
Whipped cream

Combine cocoa powder, sugar, cinnamon, and salt in a saucepan. In a separate saucepan, heat milk over medium heat until it becomes hot, not quite to a boil. Add just a few tablespoons of the hot milk into the cocoa mix, and stir into a smooth paste with a wooden spoon. Gradually add the remainder of the milk and continue stirring until fully incorporated. Simmer over low heat for 5 minutes, then froth with an immersion blender until creamy and foamy. Divide into four pre-warmed cups, and top each with whipped cream and a dusting of cinnamon.

Makes 4 servings

Chantilly Cream

The luxurious crown at the summit of a fashionable hot cocoa, "Chantilly" is whipped cream upgraded with sugar and vanilla, providing cool, sweet, fragrant contrast to the hot drink—each sip inviting part cream and part cocoa. (When Chantilly is added, less sugar should be used in the cocoa.) The frothy topping takes its name from Château de Chantilly, where it was served at extravagant banquets honoring Louis XIV who ruled France for seventy-two years.

1 cup heavy cream, well-chilled
½ teaspoon vanilla extract
1 tablespoon confectioner's sugar

Add the cream, vanilla, and sugar to the pre-chilled bowl of an electric mixer fitted with the whisk attachment, and beat until the cream is stiff and stands in firm peaks on the beater when it is lifted from the bowl. Cover Chantilly cream with plastic wrap (cream absorbs other flavors easily) and refrigerate until ready to use (within 2 hours or it will lose its volume).

Makes 8 servings

Frozen Hot Cocoa

It's a cleverly quirky culinary contradiction inspired by the signature con-fection at Serendipity 3, the legendary New York City dessert parlor. Each happiness-inducing dessert is made by combining cocoa, milk, and ice in a blender, whirring on high speed until smooth. The secret lies in mixing both natural and Dutch-process cocoas for a richer, fuller impression and com-plexity on the palate. The frosty treat is most properly served in a wide goblet meant for sharing—a romantic notion, either sipped through straws or eaten with spoons.

⅓ cup evaporated instant dry milk
⅓ cup granulated sugar
2 tablespoons unsweetened natural cocoa
2 tablespoons unsweetened Dutch-process cocoa
1 cup milk
3 cups ice
Whipped cream, for topping
Semi-sweet chocolate shavings, for garnish

Stir dry milk, sugar, and cocoa powders in a small bowl to com-bine. Add the dry mix, milk, and ice to a blender. Blend for 20 to 30 seconds until finely crushed (the consistency of a frozen daiquiri). Pour into a large goblet (for sharing) or two 16-ounce glasses. Top with whipped cream and chocolate shavings. Serve with 2 spoons and 2 straws.

Makes 2 servings

Melted Ice Cream Hot Cocoa

....

It's said you can't buy happiness—but you can buy ice cream, and that's pretty much the same thing. While it may sound a bit strange to put something cold in your hot cocoa, a scoop of melted ice cream makes it extra luscious and creamy. What flavor of ice cream, you ask? Mint chip is awesome; even plain-Jane vanilla or chocolate will do just fine.

4 rounded teaspoons unsweetened cocoa powder
1 tablespoon sugar, or to taste
1 pinch salt
1 cup whole milk
1 cup ice cream, softened
Whipped cream (optional)

Combine cocoa powder, sugar, and salt in a saucepan. In a separate saucepan, heat milk and ice cream over medium heat until it becomes hot, not quite to a boil. Add just a few tablespoons of the hot milk into the cocoa mix, and stir into a smooth paste with a wooden spoon. Gradually add the remainder of the milk and continue stirring until fully incorporated. Simmer over low heat for 5 minutes, then froth with an immersion blender until creamy and foamy. Divide into two pre-warmed cups, and top each with whipped cream if desired.

Makes 2 servings

Hot Cocoa, Mexican Style

Tracing its history to the Mayans and Aztecs, Mexican chocolate takes the form of a coarse tablet made with roasted cacao nibs and sugar, scented with cinnamon. In addition to Hispanic markets, Mexican chocolate can be found in some grocery stores in the specialty foods section. Sweetness from the sugar makes the addition of extra sweetener unnecessary. For an extra spicy drink, add a pinch of cayenne pepper to the pot while heating it up, or add it to taste at the end.

3.3 ounce tablet Mexican sweet chocolate, chopped
1 rounded teaspoon unsweetened cocoa powder
2 cups whole milk
Pinch of salt
Cayenne pepper (optional)

Combine Mexican chocolate and cocoa with ½ cup of milk and salt in medium saucepan. Heat mixture over medium heat, stirring, until chocolate melts, about 5 minutes. Add remainder of the milk and stir with a wooden spoon until fully incorporated. Simmer over low heat for 5 minutes, then froth with an immersion blender until creamy and foamy. Divide into two pre-warmed cups, and top each with whipped cream if desired.

Makes 2 servings

Morning

Malted Hot Cocoa with Toasted Marshmallows
Darkest Dark Hot Cocoa
Bed & Breakfast Vanilla Hot Cocoa
"Way of Tea" Hot Cocoa
Corn Flakes "Cereal Milk" Hot Cocoa
"Good Morning" Hot Cocoa Muffins

Malted Hot Cocoa with Toasted Marshmallows

··

Malted milk powder, made from barley malt, wheat, milk, and a smidgen of salt, dates from the late 19th century. James and William Horlick, London-born brothers who had moved to America, sold it as a dietary supplement for infants and the elderly, then as the key ingredient in soda fountain Malted Milkshakes and Dusty Road Sundaes. Its umami-like flavor profile amplifies a savory hot cocoa for breakfast, and combined with toasted marshmallows, the morning cup becomes a rich, creamy, nostalgic treat—an uplifting start to the day.

2 rounded teaspoons unsweetened cocoa powder
1 level teaspoon malted milk powder
1 level teaspoon sugar, or to taste
1 cup milk
3 toasted marshmallows*

Combine cocoa powder, malted milk powder, and sugar in your favorite cup. Place milk in a small saucepan over medium heat until it becomes hot, not quite to a boil. Add just a few tablespoons of the hot milk into the cocoa mix, and stir into a smooth paste with a wooden spoon. Gradually add the remainder of the milk and continue stirring until fully incorporated. Froth with an immersion blender until creamy and frothy. Top with toasted marshmallows.

*Heat oven broiler or toaster oven. Place 3 marshmallows on a foil-lined baking sheet and broil until golden brown and just beginning to melt.

Makes 1 serving

Darkest Dark Hot Cocoa

During Robert Falcon Scott's attempt to reach the South Pole, he had his men drink hot cocoa in the mornings to get something substantial and invigorating in their stomachs as they prepared for the march. Research shows that your body can use hot cocoa to get the day going, naturally energizing itself with the release of the adrenal hormone "cortisol" during early morning hours. The usual caffeinated, heart-throbbing morning ritual, it seems, is not indispensable after all. This drink looks like coffee, has the robust, slightly earthy notes of coffee, but without the caffeine. No crash and no jitters. A gentler, more relaxing wake-up.

1 rounded teaspoon Black Onyx cocoa powder
1 rounded teaspoon unsweetened cocoa powder
1 level teaspoon sugar, or to taste
1 pinch salt
1 cup water
milk (optional)

Combine cocoa powders, sugar, and salt in your favorite cup. Place water in a small saucepan over medium heat until it becomes hot, not quite to a boil. Add just a few tablespoons of the hot water into the cocoa mix, and stir into a smooth paste with a wooden spoon. Gradually add the remainder of the water and continue stirring until fully incorporated. Add extra sweetener and/or milk to taste preference.

Makes 1 serving

Bed & Breakfast Vanilla Hot Cocoa

A New England country inn–inspired hot cocoa becomes sophisticated with the aromatics of vanilla. Let your senses take over—since the sense of taste is not as keen as the sense of smell, a cup of cocoa literally bursts to life when partnered with "the queen of spices." Beans should be plump, pliable, and feel dense and somewhat oily. The longer the bean, the better the flavor. Each serving will make your home kitchen fragrant with sweet smells and provide a mood-lifting experience for everyone in it.

2 rounded teaspoons unsweetened cocoa powder
1 level teaspoon vanilla-infused sugar* or to taste
1 pinch salt
1 cup milk
Whipped cream (optional)

Combine cocoa powder, infused sugar, and salt in your favorite cup. Place milk in a small saucepan over medium heat until it becomes hot, not quite to a boil. Add just a few tablespoons of the hot milk into the cocoa mix, and stir into a smooth paste with a wooden spoon. Gradually add the remainder of the milk and continue stirring until fully incorporated. Froth with an immersion blender until creamy and frothy. Top with whipped cream if desired.

*Place 2 cups of sugar in large bowl. Split 1 vanilla bean lengthwise with a knife, scrape seeds into sugar, and add pod. Work seeds in with your fingers. Cover snugly with plastic wrap and let stand overnight at room temperature. Remove pod from sugar.

Makes 1 serving

"Way of Tea" Hot Cocoa

Only good things can happen when you start your day with an ancient delicacy. Matcha green tea has been used for centuries in a traditional Japanese tea ceremony known as the "Way of Tea." Shade-grown leaves are delicately ground into silky smooth, jade-green powder that adds a vegetal, earthy undertone to morning hot cocoa without overwhelming the drink. Borrowing from the Zen of ancient ceremony, the essence of Matcha becomes one with soothing cocoa to bring about a sense of peace and tranquility. Ommmm.

2 rounded teaspoons unsweetened cocoa powder
½ teaspoon Matcha green tea powder
1 level teaspoon sugar, or to taste
1 pinch salt
1 cup milk

Combine cocoa powder, green tea powder, sugar, and salt in your favorite cup. Place milk in a small saucepan over medium heat until it becomes hot, not quite to a boil. Add just a few tablespoons of the hot milk into the cocoa mix, and stir into a smooth paste with a wooden spoon. Gradually add the remainder of the milk and continue stirring until fully incorporated. Froth with an immersion blender until creamy and foamy.

Makes 1 serving

Corn Flakes "Cereal Milk" Hot Cocoa

Getting to the end is the best thing about eating cereal. Milk that's left over at the bottom of the bowl is dense and slightly sweet. You might imagine cereal milk is, you know, for kids, but this steeped and seasoned version, made fashionable by pastry chef Christina Tosi, turns plain old milk into toasted corn flake–enriched milk for a flavorsome hot cocoa.

2 rounded teaspoons unsweetened cocoa powder
1 level teaspoon sugar, or to taste
1 pinch salt
1 cup cereal milk*

Combine cocoa powder, sugar, and salt in your favorite cup. Place cereal milk in a small saucepan over medium heat until it becomes hot, not quite to a boil. Add just a few tablespoons of the hot milk into the cocoa mix, and stir into a smooth paste with a wooden spoon. Gradually add the remainder of the milk and continue stirring until fully incorporated. Froth with an immersion blender until creamy and foamy.

*Preheat oven to 300°F. Line a baking sheet with parchment paper. Spread 1 cup of corn flakes on prepared baking sheet. Transfer to oven and bake until lightly toasted, about 15 minutes. Remove from oven and let cool completely. Transfer cooled corn flakes to a large glass. Pour 1 cup of milk into the glass. Stir and let steep at room temperature for 20 minutes. Set a fine mesh strainer over a container; strain milk, pressing down on the corn flakes but taking care not to push them through the sieve. Discard solids.

Makes 1 serving

"Good Morning" Hot Cocoa Muffins

"One should always eat muffins quite calmly—it is the only way to eat them," wrote Oscar Wilde in The Importance of Being Earnest. *These muffins are easy to prepare, light as a feather, and fresh from the oven, they pack a rich, fortifying taste of cocoa to satisfy the morning appetite. They are not overly sweet, in a perfectly breakfast kind of way, an unhurried indulgence before the whirlwind of the day.*

1½ cups all-purpose flour
²⁄₃ cup unsweetened cocoa powder
⅓ cup granulated white sugar
1½ teaspoons baking powder
1 teaspoon baking soda
½ teaspoon salt
¾ cup milk
⅓ cup vegetable or canola oil
1 large egg, beaten

Preheat the oven to 400°F. Liberally grease 12 muffin tin cups with butter or coconut oil. In a medium bowl, sift together flour, cocoa powder, sugar, baking powder, baking soda, and salt. In a large bowl, whisk together milk, oil, and the egg. Add dry ingredients and stir until fully combined. Spoon the thick batter into the prepared cups, each about ²⁄₃ full. Bake 18 to 20 minutes, or until a wooden pick inserted into the center of a muffin comes out clean. Let cool for 10 minutes. Remove from muffin tin; serve warm.

Makes 12 servings

Afternoon

....

Hot Cocoa Scented with Cardamom
After-School S'mores Hot Cocoa
"Good Karma" Chai Spiced Cocoa
Peanut Butter Hot Cocoa
Clementine Hot Cocoa
Cocoa Biscotti (for Dunking)

Hot Cocoa Scented with Cardamom

....

Winter doesn't have to equal gloom. A chilly winter's afternoon is the best time to become acquainted with cardamom, a warming spice valued for its sweet, spicy fragrance. Black cardamom is dried over an open fire, providing alluring, smoky notes, and its full complexity of flavor isn't truly appreciated until mixed into a sweetened cup of hot cocoa. (Choose plump and firm pods of black cardamom to ensure they are brimming with seeds.)

2 rounded teaspoons unsweetened cocoa powder
1 level teaspoon sugar, or to taste
½ teaspoon black cardamom powder*
1 pinch salt
1 cup milk

Combine cocoa powder, sugar, cardamom powder, and salt in your favorite cup. Place milk in a small saucepan over medium heat until it becomes hot, not quite to a boil. Add just a few tablespoons of the hot milk into the cocoa mix, and stir into a smooth paste with a wooden spoon. Gradually add the remainder of the milk and continue stirring until fully incorporated. Froth with an immersion blender until creamy and foamy.

*Crack open 6 black cardamom pods and discard the shells. Grind the seeds in a spice grinder to a fine powder. Pass the ground powder through a sieve to remove the outer skin. Store in an airtight container and use as required.

Makes 1 serving

After-School S'mores Hot Cocoa

Recapture memories of a fireside treat of youth—that wonderful cold-comfort combination of Graham crackers, toasted marshmallow, and chocolate. This warm, cozy drink has all the elements of traditional S'mores, but in a drinkable, home-kitchen version. Reward the kids with an after-school hot cocoa with brûléed marshmallows, a drizzle of chocolate syrup, and bits of Graham cracker with every sip. Not only for the kids, but for everyone's "inner kid."

¼ cup Graham crackers, crushed
4 rounded teaspoons unsweetened cocoa powder
2 level teaspoons sugar, or to taste
1 pinch salt
2 cups milk
½ cup mini marshmallows
Chocolate syrup

Preheat oven to broil. Moisten the rim of 2 serving cups; dip each in Graham cracker crumbs to coat. Combine cocoa, sugar, and salt in a saucepan. In a separate saucepan, heat milk over medium heat until it becomes hot, not quite to a boil. Add just a few tablespoons of the hot milk into the cocoa mix, and stir into a smooth paste with a wooden spoon. Gradually add the remainder of the milk and continue stirring until fully incorporated. Simmer over low heat for 5 minutes, then froth with an immersion blender until creamy and foamy. Divide between the 2 prepared cups and top each with ¼ cup of marshmallows. Set mugs on a baking sheet in the oven and broil until marshmallows are golden brown. Carefully remove from the oven with a towel. Top each with extra Graham cracker crumbs and a drizzle of chocolate syrup before serving.

Makes 2 servings

"Good Karma" Chai Spiced Cocoa

Native to India, the soothing drink called "chai" is commonly made with rich black tea, milk, and a variety of exotic spices. Those same aromatic, comforting spices swirl in the air to give steaming hot cocoa a whole new lease on life, perhaps a little help getting over the afternoon hump. It is said that when we imbue chai with positive vibes during preparation, it brings blessings and good karma.

½ cup unsweetened cocoa powder
2 tablespoons sugar, or to taste
1 pinch salt
4 cups whole milk
4 star anise
1 cinnamon stick, broken into pieces
6 whole cloves
½ teaspoon white peppercorns
½ teaspoon whole allspice
¼ teaspoon fennel seeds
1 teaspoon cardamom pods, lightly crushed
3 thin slices fresh ginger
Whipped cream (optional)

Combine cocoa powder, sugar, and salt in a saucepan. In a separate saucepan, heat milk over medium heat until it becomes hot, not quite to a boil. Add just a few tablespoons of the hot milk into the cocoa mix, and stir into a smooth paste with a wooden spoon. Gradually add the remainder of the milk and continue stirring until fully incorporated. Add chai spices and simmer over low heat for 5 to 7 minutes (the longer you let it steep, the stronger the spice flavors). Strain into 4 large mugs and serve with whipped cream if desired.

Makes 4 servings

Afternoon   47

Peanut Butter Hot Cocoa

The mutual attraction of peanut butter and chocolate has been obvious since candy maker Harry Burnett Reese created a confection made of chocolate-coated peanut butter in the 1920s. Creamy and comforting, this enriched cocoa tastes like a peanut butter cup in sippable form. When peanut butter is melted into the hot cocoa, nutty flavors are released in a burst. For added indulgence, top with whipped cream and a warm peanut butter drizzle.

2 rounded teaspoons unsweetened cocoa powder
1 level teaspoon sugar, or to taste
1 pinch salt
1 cup milk
1 to 2 tablespoons smooth-style peanut butter + extra for garnish
Whipped cream

Combine cocoa powder, sugar, and salt in your favorite cup. Place milk in a small saucepan over medium heat until it becomes hot, not quite to a boil. Add just a few tablespoons of the hot milk into the cocoa mix, and stir into a smooth paste with a wooden spoon. Stir in the peanut butter, and gradually add the remainder of the milk, continuing to stir until fully incorporated. Froth with an immersion blender until creamy and foamy. Top with whipped cream and drizzle with melted peanut butter.

Makes 1 serving

Clementine Hot Cocoa

·····································

Just as the weather turns cold and snowy, the first clementines appear in grocery stores. Sour at first, these grandchildren of the mandarin orange get sweeter and sweeter throughout the winter, hitting peak flavor during the dreariest days of the year. There's no better time to warm up with a citrusy hot cocoa, and a great way to use up those leftover peels from the fruit.

2 rounded teaspoons unsweetened cocoa powder
1 level teaspoon sugar, or to taste
1 pinch salt
Peel from 1 clementine
1 cup milk

Combine cocoa powder, sugar, and salt in your favorite cup. Add clementine peel to milk in a small saucepan over medium heat and simmer for a few minutes. Once milk is just shy of boiling, discard peel. Add just a few tablespoons of the hot milk into the cocoa mix, and stir into a smooth paste with a wooden spoon. Gradually add the remainder of the milk and continue stirring until fully incorporated. Froth with an immersion blender until creamy and foamy.

Makes 1 serving

Cocoa Biscotti (for Dunking)

Cocoa-flavored biscotti are what afternoons are made for, offering an opportunity for the time-honored ritual of dunking. More of the flavor of the biscotti is released as it's dunked in the hot drink. Lower biscotti into the cocoa, letting it soak up a bit of liquid. If the biscotti is especially crumbly, put a large plate underneath the cup to catch stray drops or crumbs. With each bite, enjoy the blissful union of biscotti and cocoa combined.

2 cups all-purpose flour + a little extra for dusting
½ cup unsweetened cocoa powder
1 teaspoon baking soda
½ teaspoon salt
6 tablespoons butter, softened
1 cup sugar
2 large eggs
1 teaspoon vanilla extract
Powdered sugar, for dusting

Pre-heat the oven to 350°F. Line a 9 x 13-inch baking pan with foil or parchment paper. Sift dry ingredients (except sugar) together, and whisk to fully combine, then set aside. In a separate bowl, beat butter and sugar until creamy. Add eggs and vanilla extract and mix well. Add the flour mixture and combine to make a dough. (The dough will be slightly sticky. Add a light dusting of flour if it is too sticky to handle). Divide the dough in half. Flour your hands and form each dough ball into 6 x 1-inch logs on the baking pan, spacing them at least 2 inches apart. Lightly dust with powdered sugar. Bake for 30-35 minutes or until the tops are cracked and slightly firm to the touch. (Do not turn off the oven.)

(continued . . .)

Remove the baked logs from the oven and cool for 5 to 10 minutes in the pan. Transfer logs to a cutting board and slice diagonally—thin (½-inch) or thick (¾- to 1-inch). Return to baking pan and bake in the oven for 10 to 12 minutes or until crisped. Remove from the oven and cool completely on a wire rack. Store in airtight containers.

Makes 12 to 16 servings

Cocktail Hour

Five O'Clock Hot Cocoa (for Adults Only)
Cocoa-Nutmeg Brandy Alexander
"Cocoa Chanel" with Red Wine
Front Porch Hot Cocoa with Southern Comfort
Salted Cocoa-Dusted Almonds
"New" Mexican Hot Cocoa
with Ancho Chile, Cinnamon, and Tequila

Five O'Clock Hot Cocoa (for Adults Only)

For those who mourn an era of the civilized five o'clock tipple, happy days are here again. At the end of a workday, hot cocoa is improved with a tot of something a bit stronger for extra fortification. The combination of cocoa, sea salt, and bourbon elevates the humble cup with a perfect balance of sweet and earthy flavors. Be sure to save some "virgin" hot cocoas for the under-21 crowd.

½ **cup unsweetened cocoa powder**
2 **tablespoons sugar, or to taste**
1 **pinch Maldon sea salt**
4 **cups milk**
3 **ounces bourbon**
2 **dashes cherry bitters**
Whipped cream (optional)

Combine cocoa powder, sugar, and salt in a saucepan. In a separate saucepan, heat milk over medium heat until it becomes hot, not quite to a boil. Add just a few tablespoons of the hot milk into the cocoa mix, and stir into a smooth paste with a wooden spoon. Gradually add the remainder of the milk and continue stirring until fully incorporated. Simmer over low heat for 5 minutes, add the bourbon and cherry bitters, then froth with an immersion blender until creamy and foamy. Divide into four pre-warmed cups, and top each with whipped cream if desired.

Makes 4 servings

Cocoa-Nutmeg Brandy Alexander

A classic never goes out of style. As it happens, in this libation, the warmth of brandy slowly seeps through silky, rich cream. While a dusting of nutmeg is usually part of the ritual, the addition of cocoa powder complements the distinct chocolate flavoring of the liqueur, with sweet yet pungent aromatics. Rimming the glass provides a textural and decorative touch. The drink's complexity is slowly revealed, one sip at a time.

Rimming mix*
1½ ounces brandy
1 ounce dark crème de cacao
1 ounce fresh cream

Prepare a cocktail glass with the rimming mix. Combine brandy, crème de cacao, and cream in a mixing glass filled with cracked ice. Shake vigorously, and strain into the prepared glass.

*Place 2 tablespoons of lemon juice in a saucer. Mix together 1 teaspoon unsweetened cocoa powder, ½ teaspoon sugar, and 1 teaspoon ground nutmeg and spread on a second saucer. Carefully tip your glass toward the first saucer at about a 45-degree angle. Dip the glass into the juice, rotating the glass through the juice so that about ¼ inch of the outer edge of the rim becomes moist. Repeat the process with the glass in the second saucer, coating the outer lip of the glass with the rimming mix.

Makes 1 serving

"Cocoa Chanel" with Red Wine

Working as a singer in a French cabaret, Gabrielle Chanel acquired the name "Coco" from a popular song of the early 1900s, and she went on to change the course of fashion history. Coco believed that her favorite beverages, red wine and hot chocolate, would keep her young—and sooner or later someone was bound to combine the two. The secret of this seductive pairing is a big, fruity red wine, such as Merlot, Shiraz, or Zinfandel.

½ cup unsweetened cocoa powder
2 tablespoons sugar, or to taste
1 pinch salt
4 cups milk
6 ounces red wine
Whipped cream (optional)

Combine cocoa powder, sugar, and salt in a saucepan. In a separate saucepan, heat milk over medium heat until it becomes hot, not quite to a boil. Add just a few tablespoons of the hot milk into the cocoa mix, and stir into a smooth paste with a wooden spoon. Gradually add the remainder of the milk and continue stirring until fully incorporated. Simmer over low heat for 5 minutes, add the wine, then froth with an immersion blender until creamy and foamy. Divide into four pre-warmed cups, and top each with whipped cream if desired.

Makes 4 servings

Front Porch Hot Cocoa with Southern Comfort

A liqueur originally created by bartender Martin Wilkes Heron in 19th century New Orleans, Southern Comfort adds aromatic notes of buttered almond, baked peach cobbler, and herbs to an extra-comforting cup of hot cocoa. It's a reminder of a time when sitting on the front porch in a rocking chair and waving as the neighbors go by was practically an art form. The drink is so good, as they say in the South, it "makes your tongue want to slap your brains out."

½ cup unsweetened cocoa powder
2 tablespoons sugar, or to taste
1 pinch salt
4 cups milk
3 ounces Southern Comfort
Whipped cream (optional)

Combine cocoa powder, sugar, and salt in a saucepan. In a separate saucepan, heat milk over medium heat until it becomes hot, not quite to a boil. Add just a few tablespoons of the hot milk into the cocoa mix, and stir into a smooth paste with a wooden spoon. Gradually add the remainder of the milk and continue stirring until fully incorporated. Simmer over low heat for 5 minutes, add the Southern Comfort, then froth with an immersion blender until creamy and foamy. Divide into four pre-warmed cups, and top each with whipped cream if desired.

Makes 4 servings

Salted Cocoa-Dusted Almonds

They're ever so slightly salty and chocolatey, perfect for satisfying both sweet tooth and chocolate craving in one little almond crunch. For a party, you can make larger amounts a week or two ahead of time and store them in tightly closed jars. These crowd-pleasing tidbits pair perfectly with strong spirits at any home happy hour. Packaged in a mason jar and wrapped with a ribbon, they make a delicious edible gift.

2 cups whole raw almonds
2 tablespoons agave syrup
2 teaspoons sea salt
2 tablespoons unsweetened cocoa powder

Preheat oven to 350°F. In a large bowl combine almonds, agave, and sea salt. With a rubber spatula, mix together, fully coating the almonds. Spread almonds in a single layer on a parchment-lined baking sheet. Bake for 10 minutes, stirring twice during baking to prevent almonds from burning. Remove baking sheet from the oven. Immediately return almonds to the bowl, add cocoa powder, and toss to coat. Fully cool and store in an airtight container.

Makes 2 cups

"New" Mexican Hot Cocoa with Ancho Chile, Cinnamon, and Tequila

Mexico is known for being the first place to use cocoa beans for human enjoyment—not only for drinks, but as religious offerings, and even as a form of currency. This tipsy, tequila-spiked concoction, influenced by ingredients from the neighboring northern states of Mexico, is anything but boring. That there's harmony in the flavor notes can be a revelation. A cocktail hour treat—and some would say there's never a bad time for a little tequila.

½ cup unsweetened cocoa powder + extra for dusting
2 tablespoons sugar, or to taste
1 pinch salt
4 cinnamon sticks
1 whole dried ancho chile pod, split
2 cups milk
2 cups cream
4 ounces tequila
Whipped cream

Combine cocoa powder, sugar, and salt in a saucepan. In a separate saucepan, add cinnamon sticks and chile pod to the milk and cream over medium-low heat. Cook, stirring, for 5 minutes or until almost simmering (don't boil). Set aside, covered, for 10 minutes to let flavors develop. Strain solids and discard. Re-heat the milk and cream until it becomes hot, not quite to a boil. Add just a few tablespoons of the hot milk into the cocoa mix, and stir into a smooth paste with a wooden spoon.

(continued ...)

Gradually add the remainder of the milk and continue stirring until fully incorporated. Simmer over low heat for 5 minutes, add the tequila, then froth with an immersion blender until creamy and foamy. Divide into four pre-warmed cups. Top each with whipped cream and dust with cocoa powder.

Makes 4 servings

After Dinner

Hot Cocoa "Affogato"
"Upstairs" Hot Cocoa
Hot Cocoa with Peppermint Schnapps
Hot Cocoa Amaro
Verte Chaud
Hot Irish Mocha

Hot Cocoa "Affogato"

The fusion of hot cocoa and ice cream creates something that goes above and beyond ordinary dessert. The word "affogato" means "drowned," and this version of the Italian dish is made with ice cream generously bathed in hot cocoa. As soon as hot cocoa hits ice cream, melting begins, and the marriage of hot and cold turns ice cream into an instant float, creating a creamy, festive dinner party indulgence.

1 large scoop vanilla ice cream*
¼ cup Obligatory Hot Cocoa (page 15)
½ tablespoon Grand Marnier or Cointreau (optional)
Pinch of sea salt, such as fleur de sel

Add two scoops of ice cream to a bowl or large cup. Pour hot cocoa over the ice cream. Drizzle with liqueur if desired. Sprinkle sea salt on top.

*Substitute chocolate, mint chocolate chip, or other favorite ice cream flavor.

"Upstairs" Hot Cocoa

The popular BBC television series depicts a wealthy British household with the servants "downstairs" and their masters, the family, "upstairs." Hot cocoa laced with spices is a "must-have" for the Bellamy family and for that matter, much of British aristocratic society in Edwardian London. Turmeric and cinnamon, two of the spices British colonialists brought back from India, were commonly additions to after-dinner servings of hot cocoa as digestive relief.

½ cup unsweetened cocoa powder
1 level teaspoon turmeric
1 level teaspoon cinnamon
4 cups milk
Sugar, to taste

Combine cocoa powder, turmeric, and cinnamon in a saucepan. In a separate saucepan, heat the milk until steaming but not boiling. Add just a few tablespoons of the hot milk into the cocoa mix, and stir into a smooth paste with a wooden spoon. Gradually add the remainder of the milk and continue stirring until fully incorporated. Simmer over low heat for 5 minutes, then in British tradition, whip with a Dover egg-whip to create a foam. Divide into four pre-warmed cups, and sweeten by stirring in sugar, at the table.

Makes 4 servings

Hot Cocoa with Peppermint Schnapps

The word "schnaps" is German for "swallow." Peppermint schnapps is a clear, mint-flavored spirit sipped and swallowed after a big meal to soothe and calm the stomach. In partnership with hot cocoa, especially in the grip of winter, schnapps turns everyday hot cocoa into something rich, comforting, and smooth as silk going down. Even better when topped with a dollop of whipped cream.

½ cup unsweetened cocoa powder
2 tablespoons sugar, or to taste
1 pinch salt
4 cups milk
3 ounces peppermint schnapps
Whipped cream (optional)

Combine cocoa powder, sugar, and salt in a saucepan. In a separate saucepan, heat the milk until steaming but not boiling. Add just a few tablespoons of the hot milk into the cocoa mix, and stir into a smooth paste with a wooden spoon. Gradually add the remainder of the milk and continue stirring until fully incorporated. Simmer over low heat for 5 minutes, add the schnapps, then froth with an immersion blender until creamy and foamy. Divide into four pre-warmed cups, and top each with whipped cream if desired.

Makes 4 servings

Hot Cocoa Amaro

Italians consider a smoothly running digestive system as crucial to health and happiness. They have developed liqueurs known collectively as amari, bitter palliatives meant to counter postprandial lethargy. Amaro Averna, first produced by Salvatore Averna in 1868 in Caltanissetta, Sicily, isn't overpoweringly bitter or too sticky-sweet. It has a subtle herbal finish and a deep note of caramel, as it mingles with hot cocoa in a digestivo perfetto.

½ cup unsweetened cocoa powder
1 tablespoon sugar, or to taste
1 pinch salt
4 cups milk
3 ounces Amaro Averna
Whipped cream (optional)

Combine cocoa powder, sugar, and salt in a saucepan. In a separate saucepan, heat the milk until steaming but not boiling. Add just a few tablespoons of the hot milk into the cocoa mix, and stir into a smooth paste with a wooden spoon. Gradually add the remainder of the milk and continue stirring until fully incorporated. Simmer over low heat for 5 minutes, add the amaro, then froth with an immersion blender until creamy and foamy. Divide into four pre-warmed cups, and top each with whipped cream if desired.

Makes 4 servings

Verte Chaude

In villages of the French Alps, un tasse verte chaude is part of local tradition. At the Monkey Bar in the village of Chamonix, a resort on north side of the summit of Mont Blanc, the most popular après-ski libation is a Chartreuse-spiked rich hot cocoa, guaranteed to warm the body inside and out, finished with a "white mountain" of whipped cream. The essence of the drink is diving through the cold cream to the warm underbelly.

½ cup unsweetened cocoa powder
2 tablespoons sugar, or to taste
1 pinch salt
4 cups milk
3 ounces Green Chartreuse
Whipped cream

Combine cocoa powder, sugar, and salt in a saucepan. In a separate saucepan, heat the milk until steaming but not boiling. Add just a few tablespoons of the hot milk into the cocoa mix, and stir into a smooth paste with a wooden spoon. Gradually add the remainder of the milk and continue stirring until fully incorporated. Simmer over low heat for 5 minutes, add the Chartreuse, then froth with an immersion blender until creamy and foamy. Divide into four pre-warmed cups, and top each with whipped cream.

Makes 4 servings

Hot Irish Mocha

The original drink was invented on a stormy night in 1943 when a Pan Am flight headed from Ireland to New York was forced to turn back in bad weather. Upon return to Shannon airport, the cook warmed up passengers with whiskey-spiked coffee topped with cream. Cocoa has many notable affinities, and it blends particularly well with coffee in this riff on the classic after-dinner libation. Sipping spiked hot mocha through the cool, lightly-whipped cream is a remarkable sensation. The complementary flavors combine in a drink that doubles as dessert.

½ cup unsweetened cocoa powder
2 tablespoons sugar, or to taste
1 pinch salt
1 tablespoon milk, hot
4 cups freshly-brewed coffee, hot
2 ounces Cointreau
4 ounces Bailey's Original Irish Cream
Wet cream*

Combine cocoa powder, sugar, and salt in a saucepan. Add the hot milk into the cocoa mix, and stir into a smooth paste with a wooden spoon. Gradually add the hot coffee and continue stirring until fully incorporated. Simmer over low heat for 5 minutes, add the Cointreau and Bailey's, then froth with an immersion blender. Divide into four pre-warmed cups or Irish Coffee glasses, and top each with a collar of the wet cream by pouring gently over the back of a spoon.

*Wet cream is made in the same manner as whipped cream, but whipping stops before the cream becomes stiff. The aeration allows the cream to sit neatly on top of the hot drink.

Makes 4 servings

Bedtime

Almond Joyful Hot Cocoa
Lavender Hot Cocoa
Ginger Hot Cocoa
Hot Buttered Cocoa
Whiskey-a-Cocoa "Nightcap"
Homemade Graham Crackers

Almond Joyful Hot Cocoa

There are few things more comforting than a warm mug of cocoa before bedtime, and few ingredients more slumber-friendly than almond milk. Almonds are a rich source of magnesium, a mineral that contributes to a good night's sleep. The relaxing and soothing effect of warm milk made from ground almonds mixed with cocoa powder will help you fall asleep softly and soundly. *Better than a sleeping pill.*

2 rounded teaspoons unsweetened cocoa powder
1 level teaspoon sugar, or to taste
1 cup almond milk
Whipped cream (optional)

Combine the cocoa powder and sugar in your favorite cup. Place the almond milk in a small saucepan over medium heat until it is hot, not quite to a boil. Add just a few tablespoons of the hot milk into the cocoa mix, and stir into a smooth paste with a wooden spoon. Gradually add the remainder of the milk and continue stirring until fully incorporated. Froth with an immersion blender until creamy and foamy. Top with whipped cream if desired.

Makes 1 serving

Lavender Hot Cocoa

Sometimes a seemingly lesser ingredient can also be genuinely, intimately revelatory. In a day's end hot cocoa, one of those ingredients is culinary lavender (Lavandula angustifolia), *having the sweetest and most enchanting floral notes among all species of lavender. Its calming fragrance has long been used to decrease anxiety and agitation, slowing down the nervous system and relaxing the body and mind to improve sleep quality.*

2 rounded teaspoons unsweetened cocoa powder
1 level teaspoon sugar, or to taste
1 pinch salt
1 teaspoon culinary lavender
1 cup milk
Whipped cream (optional)

Combine the cocoa powder, sugar, and salt in your favorite cup. Place lavender in a tea infuser. Add the milk and lavender to a small saucepan over medium heat until it is hot, not quite to a boil, then reduce heat and simmer for 5 minutes. Remove the infuser and add just a few tablespoons of the hot milk into the cocoa mix, and stir into a smooth paste with a wooden spoon. Gradually add the remainder of the milk and continue stirring until fully incorporated. Froth with an immersion blender until creamy and foamy. Top with whipped cream and a decorative sprinkle of lavender if desired.

Makes 1 serving

Ginger Hot Cocoa

Some say it comes directly from the Garden of Eden. For centuries ginger has been recognized for its powerful calming and soothing properties, aiding digestion and treating stomach upsets. The marriage of fresh ginger and hot cocoa is an ideal snooze time brew with a lovely warmth and a spicy fragrance reminiscent of cloves and lemon, cedar, and mint.

1 cup milk
¼-inch piece peeled fresh ginger, sliced into 2 rounds
2 rounded teaspoons unsweetened cocoa powder
1 level teaspoon sugar, or to taste
1 pinch salt
Whipped cream (optional)

In a small saucepan heat the milk and ginger over medium heat until it is hot, and allow to simmer for 1 to 2 minutes. Combine the cocoa powder, sugar, and salt in your favorite cup. Remove ginger from the milk and increase temperature of the milk, not quite to a boil. Add just a few tablespoons of the hot milk into the cocoa mix, and stir into a smooth paste with a wooden spoon. Gradually add the remainder of the milk and continue stirring until fully incorporated. Froth with an immersion blender until creamy and foamy. Top with whipped cream if desired.

Makes 1 serving

Hot Buttered Cocoa

At the end of a long day, this creamy, frothy twist on a classic Hot Buttered Rum will relax tired muscles and comfort the weary. Adding butter to a hot cocoa may seem a bit out of the ordinary, but the spiced batter imparts a richness and extravagance that warms the hearts and hands of many a drinker on frosty nights.

½ cup unsweetened cocoa powder
2 tablespoons sugar, or to taste
1 pinch salt
4 cups milk
Buttered batter*

Combine cocoa, sugar, and salt in a saucepan. In a separate saucepan, heat the milk until steaming but not boiling. Add just a few tablespoons into the cocoa mix, and stir into a smooth paste. Gradually add remaining milk and stir until fully incorporated. Simmer for 5 minutes, then froth with an immersion blender until creamy. Divide into pre-warmed cups, and place one butter ball in each.

*For the buttered batter:

¼ cup unsalted butter, softened
⅓ cup brown sugar
¼ teaspoon ground cinnamon
⅛ teaspoon ground nutmeg
Pinch ground cloves
Pinch salt

Place all ingredients in a small bowl. Mash together with the back of a spoon or a fork until well combined, then form into 4 balls and chill while preparing cocoa.

Makes 4 servings

Whiskey-a-Cocoa "Nightcap"

A century ago, it was fashionable to wear a nightcap at bedtime. Those comfy hats locked in warmth and aided sleep. Nowadays, the concept and practice of a nightcap means something to sip while you shrug off the weight of the day, a small alcoholic potion before bed. This whiskey-spiked hot cocoa has a certain soothing, warming, and relaxing quality that can help to induce healthful, restful sleep. Think of it as an adult bedtime story.

½ **cup unsweetened cocoa powder**
2 **tablespoons sugar, or to taste**
1 **pinch salt**
4 **cups milk**
3 **ounces whiskey**
Whipped cream (optional)

Mix together cocoa powder, sugar, and salt in a saucepan. In a separate saucepan, heat the milk until steaming but not boiling. Add just a few tablespoons of the hot milk into the cocoa mix, and stir into a smooth paste with a wooden spoon. Gradually add the remainder of the milk and continue stirring until fully incorporated. Simmer for 5 minutes, add the whiskey, then froth with an immersion blender until creamy and foamy. Divide into four pre-warmed cups, and top each with whipped cream if desired.

Makes 4 servings

Homemade Graham Crackers

Nineteenth century clergyman and dietary reformer Sylvester Graham advocated hard mattresses, open windows, fresh fruits and vegetables, pure drinking water, and cheerfulness at meals. His support for home-made whole grain bread, made from wheat coarsely ground at home, inspired the digestive biscuit that bears his name. Low in fat and moderate in sugar, the crackers bring on warm, fuzzy childhood memories—the perfect companion to hot cocoa at bedtime.

8 ounces (2 sticks) unsalted butter, softened
½ cup light brown sugar, packed
2 tablespoons molasses
2 tablespoons honey
2 teaspoon ground cinnamon
1 teaspoon kosher salt
1¾ cups whole wheat flour
¾ cup all-purpose flour
2½-inch square cookie cutter

Preheat oven to 350° F. Line a sheet tray with parchment paper. Beat butter with sugar, molasses, and honey until light and fluffy, about 2 minutes. Add cinnamon, salt, and both flours, and mix until combined. Place dough between two pieces of wax paper lightly dusted with flour, and roll out to 1-inch thick. Using the square cookie cutter, cut out 24 portions and place on the lined sheet tray. Use a fork to prick three decorative lines on each cracker. Bake for 20 minutes, or until crackers begin to brown at the edges.

Makes 2 dozen crackers

Holiday Cocoa

Candy Cane Hot Cocoa
Cocoa Eggnog
Pumpkin Spice Hot Cocoa
Mulled Hot Cocoa
Maple Hot Cocoa
"Happy" Cocoa Cookies for Santa

Candy Cane Hot Cocoa

The tradition of handing out candy canes during Christmas services began in Germany, and it was a German immigrant from Wooster, Ohio, who first decorated a Christmas tree with candy canes. By the turn of the last century, candy canes were decorated with red and white stripes and flavored with peppermint. Comfort, meet joy. Bobbing for marshmallows in the lush liquid provides a playful encounter. Bring both to the holiday table—after decorating the tree, save a few candy canes to sweeten cups of hot cocoa.

½ cup unsweetened cocoa powder
1 tablespoon sugar, or to taste
1 pinch salt
Candy cane powder, to taste*
4 cups milk
Mini marshmallows
4 candy canes, for garnish

Combine cocoa powder, sugar, salt, and candy cane powder in a saucepan. In a separate saucepan, heat milk over medium heat until it becomes hot, not quite to a boil. Add just a few tablespoons of the hot milk into the cocoa mix, and stir into a smooth paste with a wooden spoon. Gradually add the remainder of the milk and continue stirring until fully incorporated. Simmer over low heat for 5 minutes, then froth with an immersion blender until creamy and foamy. Divide into four pre-warmed cups. Add mini marshmallows, and garnish each with a candy cane as an edible stirrer stick.

*Gently crush 3 candy canes into a fine powder with the flat side of a meat tenderizer. For the perfect ratio of peppermint to chocolate to suit your taste, measure crushed candy canes by the teaspoon.

Makes 4 servings

Cocoa Eggnog

Eggnog was brought to America from England, where it was commonly served at holiday parties and, as noted by an English visitor in 1866, "Christmas is not properly observed unless you brew egg nog for all comers." In a quirk of evolution, this recipe marries hot cocoa to ancestral eggnog in a rich, soulful interpretation, heightened with a magical dusting of nutmeg. The secret is freshly-grating whole nutmeg to release a warm, pleasantly bitter and musky aroma that fills the air with the fragrance of Christmas.

2 tablespoons unsweetened cocoa powder
2 cups prepared eggnog
Whipped cream
Nutmeg, freshly grated

Add cocoa powder to a small saucepan. In a separate saucepan, heat the prepared eggnog until hot. Add just a few tablespoons of the hot eggnog into the cocoa, and stir into a smooth paste with a wooden spoon. Gradually add the remainder of the eggnog and continue stirring until fully incorporated. Simmer over low heat for 5 minutes, then froth with an immersion blender until creamy and foamy. Divide into 2 warmed mugs. Top with whipped cream and dust with nutmeg.

Makes 2 servings

Pumpkin Spice Hot Cocoa

Pumpkin pies enjoy a particular status during the holidays. So far as we know, a mix of spices has been essential for baking pumpkin pies as far back as 1796, according to a recipe in the first-known American cookbook, American Cookery by Amelia Simmons. Warm spices mingling with rich hot cocoa is one telltale sign that it's the most wonderful time of the year. The cup becomes dessert when it gets dressed up with a spice-dusted dollop of whipped cream.

½ cup unsweetened cocoa powder
2 tablespoons sugar, or to taste
2 teaspoons pumpkin pie spice mix* + extra for dusting
4 cups milk
Whipped cream

Combine cocoa powder, sugar, and spice mix in a saucepan. In a separate saucepan, heat milk over medium heat until it becomes hot, not quite to a boil. Add just a few tablespoons of the hot milk into the cocoa mix, and stir into a smooth paste with a wooden spoon. Gradually add the remainder of the milk and continue stirring until fully incorporated. Simmer over low heat for 5 minutes, then froth with an immersion blender until creamy and foamy. Divide into four pre-warmed cups. Top each with whipped cream and dust with spice mix.

*In a small bowl, combine 3 tablespoons ground cinnamon, 2 teaspoons ground ginger, 2 teaspoons ground nutmeg, 1½ teaspoons ground allspice, and 1½ teaspoons ground cloves.

Makes 4 servings

Mulled Hot Cocoa

One of the reasons holiday season is everyone's favorite time of year is that it's such a feast for the senses. In particular, our sense of smell is an important memory trigger, which is why the whiff of certain aromas can take us back to childhood. One perfect way of conjuring up Christmas is by filling your home with the festive aroma of warming spices in mugs of hot cocoa.

½ **cup unsweetened cocoa powder**
2 **tablespoons sugar, or to taste**
1 **cinnamon stick**
5 **cloves**
½ **teaspoon grated nutmeg**
½ **teaspoon whole allspice**
2 **star anise**
4 **cups milk**

Combine cocoa powder and sugar in a saucepan. In a separate saucepan, add cinnamon stick, cloves, nutmeg, allspice, and star anise to the milk over medium-low heat. Cook, stirring, for 5 minutes or until almost simmering (don't boil). Set aside, covered, for 10 minutes to let flavors develop. Strain solids and discard. Re-heat the milk until it becomes hot, not quite to a boil. Add just a few tablespoons of the hot milk into the cocoa mix, and stir into a smooth paste with a wooden spoon. Gradually add the remainder of the milk and continue stirring until fully incorporated. Simmer over low heat for 5 minutes, then froth with an immersion blender until creamy and foamy. Divide into four pre-warmed glasses, and serve each with a cinnamon stick.

Makes 4 servings

Maple Hot Cocoa

When it comes to drinks, Christmas truly is the season of indulgence. Whether it's a steaming mug to take off the chill after a day of shopping or building the perfect snowman, the pure decadence of maple syrup livens up ordinary hot cocoa, sweetening each drink with confectionery sugariness and enhancing aromatics with notes of vanilla and toasted nuts.

2 rounded tablespoons unsweetened cocoa powder
1 pinch salt
1 cup milk
1 tablespoon maple syrup
Whipped cream
Granulated maple sugar

Combine cocoa powder and salt in your favorite cup. Place milk in a small saucepan over medium heat until it becomes hot, not quite to a boil. Add just a few tablespoons of the hot milk into the cocoa mix, and stir into a smooth paste with a wooden spoon. Gradually add the maple syrup and remainder of the milk and continue stirring until fully incorporated. Froth with an immersion blender until creamy and foamy. Top with whipped cream and dust with maple sugar.

Make 1 serving

"Happy" Cocoa Cookies for Santa

British children leave out sherry and mince pies, while Swedish kids leave porridge. In America, leaving a plate of cookies for Santa found its beginnings during the Great Depression, as parents taught their children the importance of giving to others during economic hardship. Today's kids happily set out a plate of cookies and a glass of milk, waking in the morning to find a few crumbs on the plate and an empty glass, confirming that Santa had paid a visit. Keep a tin of these cookies for Christmas or any winter get-together.

½ cup butter, softened
¼ cup brown sugar
¼ cup granulated sugar
1 egg
1 teaspoon vanilla extract
1 cup all-purpose flour
½ cup unsweetened cocoa powder
½ teaspoon baking soda
⅛ teaspoon salt

Preheat the oven to 350°F. Using a mixer, cream the butter, brown sugar, and granulated sugar until light and fluffy. Add egg and vanilla extract and mix until combined. In a separate bowl, sift flour, cocoa powder, baking soda, and salt. Add dry ingredients into wet ingredients and mix until fully combined. Shape into balls and place on a parchment-lined baking sheet. Bake until cookies are golden around the edges, about 18 to 20 minutes. Remove from oven, and let cool on baking sheet for 2 minutes. Transfer to a wire rack, and let cool completely. Store cookies in an airtight container at room temperature up to 1 week.

Makes 16 cookies

Reception Cocoa

Hot Cocoa for a Crowd
Homemade Marshmallows
Hot Cocoa Ice Cream
Cocoa "Great Depression" Cake
Cocoa Popcorn
Hot Cocoa with Fannie Farmer

Hot Cocoa for a Crowd

It was Milton Hershey who refined the production of cocoa powder in the Pennsylvania town that now bears his name. The result was a tastier and more soluble product, which spurred the growth of the cocoa drink industry, as the Hershey name became synonymous with chocolate products. For many years, Hershey's Cocoa was promoted in a series of booklets with recipes extolling its versatility. This unintimidating, large quantity recipe was adapted from The Hershey Recipe Book, *published in 1930.*

2 cups unsweetened cocoa powder
¼ cup sugar, or to taste
½ teaspoon salt
3 quarts milk
1 tablespoon vanilla extract

Combine cocoa powder, sugar, and salt in a large saucepan. In a separate large saucepan, heat milk over medium heat until it becomes hot, not quite to a boil. Add just a few tablespoons of the hot milk into the cocoa mix, and stir into a smooth paste with a wooden spoon. Gradually add the remainder of the milk and continue stirring until fully incorporated. Simmer over low heat for 5 minutes, whisking to blend. Remove from heat and add vanilla. Serve immediately or keep warm over very low heat for up to 2 hours. At serving time, stir; ladle into pre-warmed mugs.

Makes 12 servings

Homemade Marshmallows

First valued for medicinal properties by the ancient Egyptians, extract from mallow plant roots was sweetened with honey and used as a remedy for sore throats. By the early nineteenth century, French confectioners whipped and sweetened the sap to make the first marshmallows. Dusted in powdered sugar, these easy-to-make confections are plush, chewy, sweet, and of course, pleasurable with hot cocoa. Floating marshmallows over a steaming cup is a particularly American notion.

Powdered sugar
2 envelopes Knox gelatin
1 cup cold water
2 cups granulated sugar
¼ teaspoon salt
2 teaspoons vanilla extract

Dust the bottom of an 8- or 9-inch square pan with powdered sugar. Set aside. In a small bowl, soak gelatin in ½ cup of the cold water. Set aside. Combine granulated sugar and the second ½ cup of water in a large heavy saucepan. Cook over medium heat, stirring until dissolved. Add gelatin mixture and bring to a boil. Remove from heat. Pour into a large mixing bowl and let stand until partially cool. Add salt and vanilla extract. Beat with an electric mixer on high speed until double in volume, at least 10 minutes. Pour into prepared pan to about ½-inch thick. Set to cool and firm-up. Cut into 1½-inch squares, and roll each sticky marshmallow in powdered sugar to coat.

Makes 12 servings

Hot Cocoa Ice Cream

It's the cold-comfort food equivalent of hot cocoa—chocolate ice cream made with Dutch-processed cocoa powder (darker in color and more flavorful in ice creams). Made without eggs, this ice cream is much less rich than those made with a custard base. The lack of eggs also allows the cocoa flavor to shine through, making it light in texture yet intense in taste. A show-stopping dinner party dessert.

½ **cup unsweetened cocoa powder**
½ **cup sugar**
½ **teaspoon sea salt**
2 **cups half-and-half**
2 **cups milk**

Combine cocoa powder, sugar, and salt in a small bowl. Place the cream and milk in a medium saucepan over medium-high heat and cook, whisking occasionally to prevent scorching, until it comes to a full rolling boil. Whisk the cocoa powder mixture into the pot. Reduce heat to a simmer and continue cooking for about 2 minutes, whisking occasionally.

Remove ice cream base from heat and pour into a shallow bowl, nesting in an ice bath. Let cool for 30 to 45 minutes. Pour the base into a 2-quart pitcher, cover with plastic wrap, and place in the refrigerator to cure overnight.

The next day, remove the plastic wrap from the cream mixture and bowl. Pour the well-chilled cream mixture into the mixing container of the ice cream maker and freeze according to the manufacturer's instructions. Use a rubber spatula to transfer the ice cream to a plastic freezer container. Cover tightly and place in the freezer until the ice cream is firm, at least 4 hours.

Makes 1½ quarts

Cocoa "Great Depression" Cake

It was a special treat that brightened the dinner table during the hard times of the Great Depression. Back in the day, milk, sugar, butter, and eggs were either too expensive or just plain hard to get. The Betty Crocker Cooking School of the Air *provided radio listeners with resourceful, budget-friendly recipes, including "the most worthwhile cake ever made," using water in place of milk, baking soda for eggs, and vegetable oil instead of butter. This moist, dairy-free recipe bakes into a chocolate cake that's just as delicious in an age of prosperity.*

1½ cups all-purpose flour
1 cup sugar
¼ cup unsweetened cocoa powder
½ teaspoon salt
1 teaspoon baking soda
1 teaspoon vanilla extract
1 teaspoon white vinegar
⅓ cup vegetable oil
1 cup water
Powdered sugar, for dusting

Pre-heat oven to 350°F. Combine flour, sugar, cocoa powder, salt, and baking soda in a large mixing bowl. In a separate bowl, combine vanilla, vinegar, oil, and water. Add wet ingredients to dry ingredients and mix until fully combined and no lumps remain. Pour batter into a greased 8 x 8-inch square pan. Bake for 30–35 minutes, until toothpick inserted in center comes out clean. Remove cake to a wire rack to cool. When cooled, cut into squares and sift powdered sugar over the top.

Makes 10 to 12 servings

Cocoa Popcorn

Enjoy everyone's beloved movie theater snack at home—but with a twist. It's safe to say that buttered popcorn is going to seem ordinary after munching on this cocoa-dusted version. Because the cocoa mixture sticks to the hot popcorn, it's not messy at all. Make some to snack on while watching TV, or pop a batch to enjoy anytime cravings strike.

2 tablespoons unsweetened cocoa powder
1 teaspoon organic sugar
½ teaspoon salt
1 tablespoon canola oil
¼ cup popcorn kernels

Mix the cocoa powder, sugar, and salt in a small bowl and set aside. Add the oil to a pot with a couple kernels with the top on. Turn heat on high. When the kernels begin to pop, quickly pour in the remaining kernels, and put the top on. Shake the pan from side to side, and when the popping slows down, turn off the heat and pour the popcorn in a bowl. Immediately sprinkle on the cocoa mixture and stir to combine.

Makes 4 servings

Hot Cocoa with Fannie Farmer

A wise old bird, Fannie Farmer left her imprint on cocoa culture. She came early to the benefits of hot cocoa, and in 1886, published a cookbook that was one of the first to advocate exact measurements, instead of a pinch of this, a handful of that. It became a best-seller across America, selling over 4 million copies during her lifetime. As director of the Boston Cooking School, she taught nurses at Harvard Medical School to serve hot cocoa as a remedy for stomach maladies. Ms. Farmer, who added brandy to flavor many of her recipes, was known to take an occasional nip in the kitchen.

½ cup unsweetened cocoa powder
2 tablespoons sugar, or to taste
1 pinch salt
4 cups milk
3 ounces brandy

Combine cocoa powder, sugar, and salt in a saucepan. In a separate saucepan, heat milk over medium heat until it becomes hot, not quite to a boil. Add just a few tablespoons of the hot milk into the cocoa mix, and stir into a smooth paste with a wooden spoon. Gradually add the remainder of the milk and continue stirring until fully incorporated. Simmer over low heat for 5 minutes. Add the brandy, then froth with an immersion blender until creamy and foamy. Divide into four pre-warmed cups.

Makes 4 servings

Whipped Cream Menu

Cool, lightly-sweetened whipped cream adds dimension, tempers richness, and furnishes a measure of grace to hot cocoa.

The fluffy cloud, of course, is nothing more than air bubbles beaten into heavy cream. So please don't settle for prepackaged products or, heaven forbid, imitation "whipped topping" out of a pressurized can.

To start, make sure the cream is very cold, straight from the refrigerator. Chilling the bowl and whisk also aids in achieving full volume. Whip the cold cream with a hand beater or an electric mixer at moderate speed until the cream is slightly thickened. This is the correct time to add sugar or other flavoring ingredients. Continue whipping until cream forms distinct mounds that hold their shape. Whipping beyond the soft-peak stage will cause the cream to become stiff and curdle.

To sweeten, always use confectioner's sugar, never granulated sugar. Confectioner's dissolves faster, avoiding gritty topping. Flavorings can range from extracts, chocolate, coffee, citrus zest, or spices, to bourbon, rum, brandy, or other liqueurs. As the whipped cream melts, flavors soften and marry into a more savory drink.

Basic Whipped Cream

1 cup heavy cream, well-chilled
2 tablespoons confectioner's sugar, or to taste
½ teaspoon vanilla extract

Add the cream to mixing bowl and whip until the cream is slightly thickened. Add the sugar and vanilla, and continue whipping until cream holds its shape. Spoon on top of hot cocoa.

Makes 8 servings

Chocolate Whipped Cream

1 cup heavy cream, well-chilled
¼ cup unsweetened Dutch-processed cocoa powder
2 tablespoons confectioner's sugar, or to taste
½ teaspoon vanilla extract

Add the cream to mixing bowl and whip until the cream is slightly thickened. Add the sugar and vanilla; gradually pour in cocoa powder. Continue whipping until cream holds its shape. Spoon on top of hot cocoa. (For an "Upside-Down Hot Cocoa," fill a cup with warm milk and spoon chocolate whipped cream on top.)

Makes 8 servings

Cinnamon Whipped Cream

1 cup heavy cream, well-chilled
2 tablespoons confectioner's sugar, or to taste
½ teaspoon vanilla extract
1 teaspoon ground cinnamon

Add the cream to mixing bowl and whip until the cream is slightly thickened. Add the sugar, vanilla, and cinnamon, and continue whipping until cream holds its shape. Spoon on top of hot cocoa.

Makes 8 servings

Bourbon Whipped Cream

1 cup heavy cream, well-chilled
1 tablespoon confectioner's sugar, or to taste
½ teaspoon vanilla extract
2 teaspoons bourbon

Add the cream to mixing bowl and whip until the cream is slightly thickened. Add the sugar, vanilla, and bourbon, and continue whipping until cream holds its shape. Spoon on top of hot cocoa.

Makes 8 servings

Cayenne Whipped Cream

1 cup heavy cream, well-chilled
2 tablespoons confectioner's sugar, or to taste
½ teaspoon vanilla extract
1 pinch cayenne pepper

Add the cream to mixing bowl and whip until the cream is slightly thickened. Add the sugar, vanilla, and cayenne, and continue whipping until cream holds its shape. Spoon on top of hot cocoa.

Makes 8 servings

Angostura Whipped Cream

1 cup heavy cream, well-chilled
1 tablespoon simple syrup, or to taste
1 teaspoon vanilla extract
6 dashes Angostura bitters

Add the cream to mixing bowl and whip until the cream is slightly thickened. Add the simple syrup, vanilla, and bitters, and continue whipping until cream holds its shape. Spoon on top of hot cocoa.

Makes 8 servings

Conversion Chart

Metric and Imperial Conversions

(These conversions are rounded for convenience)

Ingredient	Cups/ Tablespoons/ Teaspoons	Ounces	Grams/ Milliliters
Fruit, dried	1 cup	4 ounces	120 grams
Fruits or veggies, chopped	1 cup	5 to 7 ounces	145 to 200 grams
Fruits or veggies, puréed	1 cup	8.5 ounces	245 grams
Honey, maple syrup, or corn syrup	1 tablespoon	0.75 ounce	20 grams
Liquids: cream, milk, water, or juice	1 cup	8 fluid ounces	240 milliliters
Salt	1 teaspoon	0.2 ounces	6 grams
Spices: cinnamon, cloves, ginger, or nutmeg (ground)	1 teaspoon	0.2 ounce	5 milliliters
Sugar, brown, firmly packed	1 cup	7 ounces	200 grams
Sugar, white	1 cup/ 1 tablespoon	7 ounces/0.5 ounce	200 grams/12.5 grams
Vanilla extract	1 teaspoon	0.2 ounce	4 grams

Liquids

8 fluid ounces = 1 cup = ½ pint
16 fluid ounces = 2 cups = 1 pint
32 fluid ounces = 4 cups = 1 quart
128 fluid ounces = 16 cups = 1 gallon

Index

About the Author

Michael Turback created and nurtured the eponymous Turback's of Ithaca, one of Upstate New York's first destination restaurants. His mission combined inventiveness, passionate cooking with local ingredients, and the novel concept of a wine list with exclusively New York regional wines, an achievement recognized nationally. Michael was a locavore before the term existed; his loyalty to small local farmers and use of seasonal local produce helped to spark the local food movement. Cocktail programs developed in his establishments have influenced the beverage business for over three decades. He was among the first to revive and re-imagine vintage formulas, influencing a generation of "craft bartenders," and elevating mixology to a culinary art.

Michael's other titles for Skyhorse Publishing include:

> *Cocktails at Dinner: Daring Pairings of Delicious Dishes and Enticing Mixed Drinks*
>
> *ReMixology: Classic Cocktails, Reconsidered and Reinvented*
>
> *What a Swell Party It Was: Rediscovering Food & Drink from the Golden Age of the American Nightclub*